G IS FOR GEORGIA!

WRITTEN BY STACEY THOMPSON
ILLUSTRATED BY SKYLAR THOMPSON

AI-assisted tools were used to enhance select original illustrations in this book. All final images were reviewed and approved by the author.

THIS BOOK IS DEDICATED TO ALL OF MY GEORGIA FRIENDS WHO HAVE GROWN UP WITH THESE EXPERIENCES AND HAVE SHARED THEM WITH ME. ALTHOUGH WE MAY NOT SEE EYE TO EYE DURING FOOTBALL SEASON WE CAN ALL AGREE THAT GEORGIA IS MAGICAL.

A

A is for azaleas! The rich colored flower has been designated as Georgia's wildflower. You can see them in most yards around the state. A is also for Augusta, the Alman Brothers (from Macon), Athens (home of the Dawgs) and the famous Appalachian trailhead that starts in Fannin County and heads north. Whew, they must like their A's.

B

B is for the Brown Thrasher the state bird of Georgia. It was selected to be the state bird in 1939 by then Governor Eugene Talmadge. B is also for the Black Crowes straight out of Marietta!

C

C IS FOR CUMBERLAND ISLAND! WHO CAN'T GET EXCITED FOR THE WILD HORSES THAT RUN FREE ON SUCH A BEAUTIFUL ISLAND SETTING? YOU CAN ALSO FIND OTHER GREAT THINGS THAT START WITH C LIKE THE CITY OF CANTON, THE COOLEST LITTLE TOWN IN THE STATE, THE HEADQUARTERS OF COCA COLA AND YOU MIGHT GET TO HEAR THE BAND COLLECTIVE SOUL WHILE YOU'RE THERE. SO MUCH TALENT!

D

D IS FOR DRIFTWOOD THAT YOU CAN SEE ON MOST GEORGIA BEACHES. D IS ALSO FOR DOGWOOD! THE ANNUAL DOGWOOD FESTIVAL IS HELD IN MIDTOWN, ATLANTA'S PIEDMONT PARK. YOU CAN ALSO SEE DOGWOODS BLOOMING ALL OVER THE STATE OF GEORGIA FROM MARCH TO MAY.

E

E IS FOR ELLIJAY! WHEN YOU THINK OF FALL IN GEORGIA NOT ONLY DO YOU THINK ABOUT THE BEAUTIFUL TURNING LEAVES BUT ALSO THE TOWN OF ELLIJAY. VISIT THIS QUAINT LITTLE TOWN TO PICK APPLES IN SEPTEMBER AND PUMPKINS IN OCTOBER.

F

F IS FOR FALCON! NOT JUST THE FOOTBALL TEAM, BUT THE MAJESTIC BIRDS OF PREY THAT CALL GEORGIA HOME. IF YOU ARE FEELING LIKE SEEING THE CITY, VISIT THE FOX THEATER TO SEE A BALLET OR A BROADWAY ACT!

G

G IS FOR GEORGIA! IT'S ALSO FOR GONE WITH THE WIND—THE AUTHOR MARGARET MITCHELL CALLED GEORGIA HOME. G IS ALSO FOR GRITS—THE STATE FOOD.

H IS FOR HELEN! HELEN IS A QUAINT LITTLE TOWN THAT FEELS LIKE YOU ARE STEPPING INTO A GERMAN VILLAGE. YOU CAN ALSO TUBE DOWN THE FAMOUS CHATTAHOOCHEE RIVER WHEN IT'S HOT OUTSIDE. H IS ALSO FOR HOME DEPOT, HANK AARON AND HAPEVILLE, THE HOME OF CHICK-FIL-A.

I

I IS FOR ISLE OF HOPE! IN ISLE OF HOPE, THERE ARE HISTORIC HOMES AND WHITE PICKET FENCES ALL ALONG THE SKIDAWAY RIVER AND THE COASTLINE OF GEORGIA.

J

J IS FOR JEKYLL ISLAND! JEKYLL ISLAND HAS HISTORY, BEACHES WITH DRIFTWOOD AND COUNTLESS ACTIVITIES LIKE BIKE RIDING TRAILS WHERE YOU MIGHT OR MIGHT NOT RUN INTO AN ALLIGATOR, MAYBE..... J IS ALSO FOR A FEW FAMOUS PEOPLE LIKE PRESIDENT JIMMY CARTER AND ALAN JACKSON.

K

K IS FOR KENNESAW NATIONAL BATTLEFIELD! RECOGNIZED AS A NATIONAL PARK, KENNESAW NATIONAL BATTLEFIELD IS THE SITE OF THE CIVIL WAR FROM JUNE 1864 TO JULY 1864. YOU CAN DRIVE TO THE TOP OF THE MOUNTAIN OR HIKE TO THE TOP OF THE MOUNTAIN. YOU MIGHT EVEN SEE A SOLDIER OR TWO WHILE YOU ARE VISITING SHOOTING ONE OF THE CANNONS! K IS ALSO FOR KING GEORGE II WHO GRANTED THE CHARTER FOR GEORGIA IN 1732.

L

L IS FOR THE LAST ORIGINAL COLONY. GEORGIA IS THE 13TH AND THE LAST ORIGINAL COLONY. WHAT AN AMAZING HISTORY!

M

M IS FOR MARIETTA! MARIETTA, GA IS A HISTORICAL TOWN THAT SITS AT THE BASE OF KENNESAW MOUNTAIN. MARIETTA IS FULL OF ITS OWN HISTORY AND HAS ONE OF THE PRETTIEST SQUARES AROUND THE STATE. M IS ALSO FOR MARTIN LUTHER KING, JR. WHO WAS BORN AND RAISED IN ATLANTA.

N IS FOR THE NORTH GEORGIA MOUNTAINS; COMING OVER THE HILLS OF I-575 YOU CAN SEE THE BLUE RIDGE MOUNTAINS WHICH FORM PART OF THE NORTH GEORGIA MOUNTAINS. WATERFALLS AND GORGES LAYER IN AND OUT OF THE HILLS MAKING IT A BEAUTIFUL PLACE TO HIKE AND EXPLORE.

O

O IS FOR THE OKEFENOKEE SWAMP! THE OKEFENOKEE SWAMP IS A DIVERSE WETLAND THAT BEARS BLACKWATER. WHEN CANOEING OR KAYAKING YOU WILL SEE MANY SPECIES OF ANIMALS INCLUDING THE AMERICAN ALLIGATOR AND SEVERAL HUNDRED SPECIES OF BIRDS.

P

P IS FOR PEACHES! YES, I GET MY PEACHES DOWN IN GEORGIA. THERE ARE ABOUT 71 PEACHTREE STREETS, ROADS, PARKWAYS, ETC. IN THE ATLANTA AREA ALONE. GEORGIA IS AFFECTIONATELY CALLED "THE PEACH STATE".

Q IS FOR QUIRKY! ALL I SHOULD SAY IS CABBAGE PATCH KIDS AND LEAVE IT AT THAT. HOWEVER, BABYLAND GENERAL HOSPITAL IS A REAL THING IN A REAL CITY CALLED CLEVELAND, GEORGIA. IT IS ALSO ILLEGAL TO KEEP A DONKEY IN A BATHTUB IN GEORGIA, AND IT IS ILLEGAL TO TIE A GIRAFFE TO A TELEPHONE POLE IN GEORGIA.

R

R IS FOR ROSA LAEVIGATA OR THE CHEROKEE ROSE. IT IS THE GEORGIA STATE FLOWER. R IS ALSO FOR RAY CHARLES AND RHINE, GEORGIA THE WATERMELON CAPITAL OF THE WORLD.

S

S IS FOR SAVANNAH AND SPANISH MOSS! S IS ALSO FOR SOUTHERN BELLES, SOUTHERN HOSPITALITY AND ST. SIMON ISLAND. WHEW, THANK GOODNESS FOR THE SOUTH!

T

T IS FOR TYBEE ISLAND! TYBEE ISLAND IS HOME TO GEORGIA'S TALLEST AND OLDEST LIGHTHOUSES. IT IS ALSO HOME TO BEAUTIFUL BEACHES AND MANY SEA TURTLE NESTING SITES. T IS ALSO FOR THUNDERSTORMS IN JUNE THAT ARE SO FAMILIAR.

U IS FOR UNIQUE! DID YOU KNOW THERE WAS A HOLLYWOOD OF THE SOUTH? DID YOU ALSO KNOW THAT GEORGIA WAS THE FIRST STATE TO LET 18-YEAR-OLDS TO VOTE? THIS WAS ESTABLISHED IN 1945.

V

V is for Vidalia! The Vidalia onion is only grown in certain regions of Georgia. Seriously, only 20 counties outlined by the Vidalia Onion Act of 1986 are allowed to grow this onion. You will also find a certain burger place known to locals as "What'll Ya Have?".

W

W IS FOR WHITETAIL DEER THE STATE ANIMAL! W IS ALSO FOR THE HOME OF WAFFLE HOUSE, WATERFALLS AND WARM SPRINGS.

X

X is for X marks the spot! There is a historical hunt for lost Confederate gold. Make your way to Washington, Georgia and see the story for yourself.

Y

Y IS FOR YELLOW JACKETS! IN THE MIDDLE OF ATLANTA THERE IS A NEAT SCHOOL THAT USES A YELLOWJACKET AS THEIR MASCOT, HOWEVER IT WASN'T ALWAYS THE BUG. THEY STARTED WITH LITERAL YELLOW JACKETS, AND IT STUCK!

Z

Z IS FOR THE ZOO IN ATLANTA! IT IS CALLED ZOO ATLANTA, AND IT IS NESTLED IN HISTORIC GRANT PARK. IT'S A QUAINT LOCATION WITH SO MANY ANIMALS TO SEE AND LEARN ABOUT. THERE ARE OVER 20 DIFFERENT EVENTS THROUGHOUT THE YEAR INCLUDING BOO AT THE ZOO AND ZOO YEAR'S EVE.

GEORGIA HAS A LITTLE BIT OF EVERYTHING PACKED INTO A SMALL HISTORICAL STATE. FROM SOUTHERN HOSPITALITY TO SOUTHERN BELLES, FROM MOUNTAINS TO CITIES AND THEN TO OCEANS, THERE'S SOMETHING FOR EVERYONE TO LOVE.

Made in the USA
Coppell, TX
28 June 2026

83075177R00019